This Journal Belongs to

_____
_____

Dedication

This 50 States Traveled Journal is dedicated to all the travelers out there who want to travel all 50 states and document their findings in the process.

You are my inspiration for producing books and I'm honored to be a part of keeping all of your 50 States Traveled notes and records organized.

This journal notebook will help you record your details about your travel adventures.

Thoughtfully put together with these sections to record in detail: How long you stayed, Where you stayed, Weather, Best Meal, Something funny, Something unexpected, Highlights, New Friends, Notes, etc.

How to Use this Book

The purpose of this book is to keep all of your 50 States Traveled notes all in one place. It will help keep you organized.

This 50 States Traveled Journal will allow you to accurately document every detail about your 50 states journey. It's a great way to chart your course through the 50 States Challenge.

Here are examples of the prompts for you to fill in and write about your experience in this book:

1. How Long You Stayed - Write how long your trip was.
2. Where You Stayed - Log the place you stayed.
3. Weather - Record what the weather was like.
4. Best Meal - Write what your best meal of the trip was.
5. Something Funny - Log anything funny that happened.
6. Something Unexpected - Record something that happened that was unexpected.
7. Highlights of the Trip - Write the highlights of your trip.
8. What Did You Learn - Log anything you may have learned.
9. Did You Make New Friends - Record any new friends you made.
10. Why Did You Visit The State - Write why you came to the state.
11. Notes - Blank lined notes for writing memories, fun things you did on vacation or just traveling through, etc.
12. Rating of the State - Rate the state from 1-10.

Alabama

Places I Visited

- [ ]
- [ ]
- [ ]
- [ ]
- [ ]
- [ ]

Date Arrived:

Time Arrived:

How long was my stay?

Where did I stay?

Who Did I stay with?

Who Did I Travel With?

How was the weather?

Best Meal

Something Funny That Happened

Something Unexpected That Happened

Highlights of my Trip

Did I Learn Anything?   Did I Make New Friends?

Why Did I Visit This State?

Notes

I Love This State (Rating 1-10)   1 2 3 4 5 6 7 8 9 10

Alaska

Places I Visited

- [ ]
- [ ]
- [ ]
- [ ]
- [ ]
- [ ]

Date Arrived:

Time Arrived:

How long was my stay?

Where did I stay?

Who Did I stay with?

Who Did I Travel With?

How was the weather?

Best Meal

Something Funny That Happened

Something Unexpected That Happened

Highlights of my Trip

-
-
-
-
-
-

Did I Learn Anything?

Did I Make New Friends?

Why Did I Visit This State?

Notes

I Love This State (Rating 1-10)   1 2 3 4 5 6 7 8 9 10

Arizona

Places I Visited

- [ ]
- [ ]
- [ ]
- [ ]
- [ ]
- [ ]

Date Arrived:

Time Arrived:

How long was my stay?

Where did I stay?

Who Did I stay with?

Who Did I Travel With?

How was the weather?

Best Meal

Something Funny That Happened

Something Unexpected That Happened

Highlights of my Trip

☐
☐
☐
☐
☐
☐

Did I Learn Anything?

Did I Make New Friends?

Why Did I Visit This State?

Notes

I Love This State (Rating 1-10)   1 2 3 4 5 6 7 8 9 10

Arkansas

Places I Visited

- [ ]
- [ ]
- [ ]
- [ ]
- [ ]
- [ ]

Date Arrived:

Time Arrived:

How long was my stay?

Where did I stay?

Who Did I stay with?

Who Did I Travel With?

How was the weather?

Best Meal

Something Funny That Happened

Something Unexpected That Happened

Highlights of my Trip

-
-
-
-
-
-

Did I Learn Anything?

Did I Make New Friends?

Why Did I Visit This State?

Notes

I Love This State (Rating 1-10)   1 2 3 4 5 6 7 8 9 10

California

Places I Visited

- [ ]
- [ ]
- [ ]
- [ ]
- [ ]
- [ ]

Date Arrived:

Time Arrived:

How long was my stay?

Where did I stay?

Who Did I stay with?

Who Did I Travel With?

How was the weather?

Best Meal

Something Funny That Happened

Something Unexpected That Happened

Highlights of my Trip

☐

☐

☐

☐

☐

☐

Did I Learn Anything?   Did I Make New Friends?

Why Did I Visit This State?

Notes

I Love This State (Rating 1-10)   1 2 3 4 5 6 7 8 9 10

Colorado

Places I Visited

- [ ]
- [ ]
- [ ]
- [ ]
- [ ]
- [ ]

Date Arrived:

Time Arrived:

How long was my stay?

Where did I stay?

Who Did I stay with?

Who Did I Travel With?

How was the weather?

Best Meal

Something Funny That Happened

Something Unexpected That Happened

USA

Highlights of my Trip

- ☐
- ☐
- ☐
- ☐
- ☐
- ☐

Did I Learn Anything?

Did I Make New Friends?

Why Did I Visit This State?

Notes

I Love This State (Rating 1-10)   1   2   3   4   5   6   7   8   9   10

Connecticut

Places I Visited

- [ ]
- [ ]
- [ ]
- [ ]
- [ ]
- [ ]

Date Arrived:

Time Arrived:

How long was my stay?

Where did I stay?

Who Did I stay with?

Who Did I Travel With?

How was the weather?

Best Meal

Something Funny That Happened

Something Unexpected That Happened

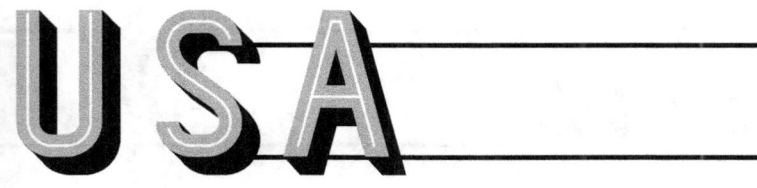

Highlights of my Trip

- ☐
- ☐
- ☐
- ☐
- ☐
- ☐

Did I Learn Anything?

Did I Make New Friends?

Why Did I Visit This State?

Notes

I Love This State (Rating 1-10)   1   2   3   4   5   6   7   8   9   10

Delaware

Places I Visited

Date Arrived:

Time Arrived:

How long was my stay?

Where did I stay?

Who Did I stay with?

Who Did I Travel With?

How was the weather?

Best Meal

Something Funny That Happened

Something Unexpected That Happened

USA

Highlights of my Trip

- ☐
- ☐
- ☐
- ☐
- ☐
- ☐

Did I Learn Anything?

Did I Make New Friends?

Why Did I Visit This State?

Notes

I Love This State (Rating 1-10)   1 2 3 4 5 6 7 8 9 10

Florida

Places I Visited

- [ ]
- [ ]
- [ ]
- [ ]
- [ ]
- [ ]

Date Arrived:

Time Arrived:

How long was my stay?

Where did I stay?

Who Did I stay with?

Who Did I Travel With?

How was the weather?

Best Meal

Something Funny That Happened

Something Unexpected That Happened

Highlights of my Trip

-
-
-
-
-
-

Did I Learn Anything?   Did I Make New Friends?

Why Did I Visit This State?

Notes

I Love This State (Rating 1-10)   1 2 3 4 5 6 7 8 9 10

Georgia

Places I Visited

- [ ]
- [ ]
- [ ]
- [ ]
- [ ]
- [ ]

Date Arrived:

Time Arrived:

How long was my stay?

Where did I stay?

Who Did I stay with?

Who Did I Travel With?

How was the weather?

Best Meal

Something Funny That Happened

Something Unexpected That Happened

Highlights of my Trip

-
-
-
-
-
-

Did I Learn Anything?

Did I Make New Friends?

Why Did I Visit This State?

Notes

I Love This State (Rating 1-10)   1 2 3 4 5 6 7 8 9 10

Hawaii

Places I Visited

- [ ]
- [ ]
- [ ]
- [ ]
- [ ]
- [ ]

Date Arrived:
Time Arrived:

How long was my stay?

Where did I stay?

Who Did I stay with?

Who Did I Travel With?

How was the weather?

Best Meal

Something Funny That Happened

Something Unexpected That Happened

Highlights of my Trip

- [ ]
- [ ]
- [ ]
- [ ]
- [ ]
- [ ]

Did I Learn Anything?   Did I Make New Friends?

_____   _____
_____   _____
_____   _____

Why Did I Visit This State?

_____
_____

Notes

_____
_____

I Love This State (Rating 1-10)   1 2 3 4 5 6 7 8 9 10

Idaho

Places I Visited

- [ ]
- [ ]
- [ ]
- [ ]
- [ ]
- [ ]

Date Arrived:

Time Arrived:

How long was my stay?

Where did I stay?

Who Did I stay with?

Who Did I Travel With?

How was the weather?

Best Meal

Something Funny That Happened

Something Unexpected That Happened

Highlights of my Trip

Did I Learn Anything? Did I Make New Friends?

Why Did I Visit This State?

Notes

I Love This State (Rating 1-10)   1 2 3 4 5 6 7 8 9 10

Places I Visited

- [ ]
- [ ]
- [ ]
- [ ]
- [ ]
- [ ]

How was the weather?

Date Arrived:
Time Arrived:

How long was my stay?

Where did I stay?

Who Did I stay with?

Who Did I Travel With?

Best Meal

Something Funny That Happened

Something Unexpected That Happened

Highlights of my Trip

Did I Learn Anything?

Did I Make New Friends?

Why Did I Visit This State?

Notes

I Love This State (Rating 1-10)   1 2 3 4 5 6 7 8 9 10

Indiana

Places I Visited

Date Arrived:

Time Arrived:

How long was my stay?

Where did I stay?

Who Did I stay with?

Who Did I Travel With?

How was the weather?

Best Meal

Something Funny That Happened

Something Unexpected That Happened

Highlights of my Trip

- [ ]
- [ ]
- [ ]
- [ ]
- [ ]
- [ ]

Did I Learn Anything? Did I Make New Friends?

_____ _____
_____ _____
_____ _____

Why Did I Visit This State?

_____
_____

Notes

_____

I Love This State (Rating 1-10)   1 2 3 4 5 6 7 8 9 10

Iowa

Places I Visited

- [ ]
- [ ]
- [ ]
- [ ]
- [ ]
- [ ]

Date Arrived:

Time Arrived:

How long was my stay?

Where did I stay?

Who Did I stay with?

Who Did I Travel With?

How was the weather?

Best Meal

Something Funny That Happened

Something Unexpected That Happened

Highlights of my Trip

- ☐
- ☐
- ☐
- ☐
- ☐
- ☐

Did I Learn Anything? Did I Make New Friends?

Why Did I Visit This State?

Notes

I Love This State (Rating 1-10)   1 2 3 4 5 6 7 8 9 10

Kansas

Places I Visited

- [ ]
- [ ]
- [ ]
- [ ]
- [ ]
- [ ]

Date Arrived: _____

Time Arrived: _____

How long was my stay?
_____
_____

Where did I stay?
_____
_____
_____

Who Did I stay with?
_____
_____
_____

Who Did I Travel With?
_____
_____

How was the weather?
_____
_____
_____

Best Meal
_____
_____

Something Funny That Happened
_____
_____

Something Unexpected That Happened
_____
_____

Highlights of my Trip

- ☐
- ☐
- ☐
- ☐
- ☐
- ☐

Did I Learn Anything?

Did I Make New Friends?

Why Did I Visit This State?

Notes

I Love This State (Rating 1-10)   1 2 3 4 5 6 7 8 9 10

Kentucky

Places I Visited

- [ ]
- [ ]
- [ ]
- [ ]
- [ ]
- [ ]

Date Arrived:

Time Arrived:

How long was my stay?

Where did I stay?

Who Did I stay with?

Who Did I Travel With?

How was the weather?

Best Meal

Something Funny That Happened

Something Unexpected That Happened

Highlights of my Trip

-
-
-
-
-
-

Did I Learn Anything?

Did I Make New Friends?

Why Did I Visit This State?

Notes

I Love This State (Rating 1-10)   1 2 3 4 5 6 7 8 9 10

Louisiana

Places I Visited

- [ ]
- [ ]
- [ ]
- [ ]
- [ ]
- [ ]

Date Arrived:

Time Arrived:

How long was my stay?

Where did I stay?

Who Did I stay with?

Who Did I Travel With?

How was the weather?

Best Meal

Something Funny That Happened

Something Unexpected That Happened

Highlights of my Trip

- ☐
- ☐
- ☐
- ☐
- ☐
- ☐

Did I Learn Anything?   Did I Make New Friends?

Why Did I Visit This State?

Notes

I Love This State (Rating 1-10)   1 2 3 4 5 6 7 8 9 10

Maine

Places I Visited

- [ ]
- [ ]
- [ ]
- [ ]
- [ ]
- [ ]

Date Arrived:
Time Arrived:

How long was my stay?

Where did I stay?

Who Did I stay with?

Who Did I Travel With?

How was the weather?

Best Meal

Something Funny That Happened

Something Unexpected That Happened

Highlights of my Trip

- [ ]
- [ ]
- [ ]
- [ ]
- [ ]
- [ ]

Did I Learn Anything?

Did I Make New Friends?

Why Did I Visit This State?

Notes

I Love This State (Rating 1-10)   1   2   3   4   5   6   7   8   9   10

Maryland

Places I Visited

- [ ]
- [ ]
- [ ]
- [ ]
- [ ]
- [ ]

Date Arrived:

Time Arrived:

How long was my stay?

Where did I stay?

Who Did I stay with?

Who Did I Travel With?

How was the weather?

Best Meal

Something Funny That Happened

Something Unexpected That Happened

Highlights of my Trip

-
-
-
-
-
-

Did I Learn Anything?

Did I Make New Friends?

Why Did I Visit This State?

Notes

I Love This State (Rating 1-10)   1 2 3 4 5 6 7 8 9 10

Massachusetts

Places I Visited

- [ ]
- [ ]
- [ ]
- [ ]
- [ ]
- [ ]

Date Arrived:

Time Arrived:

How long was my stay?

Where did I stay?

Who Did I stay with?

Who Did I Travel With?

How was the weather?

Best Meal

Something Funny That Happened

Something Unexpected That Happened

Highlights of my Trip

- ☐
- ☐
- ☐
- ☐
- ☐
- ☐

Did I Learn Anything?   Did I Make New Friends?

Why Did I Visit This State?

Notes

I Love This State (Rating 1-10)   1 2 3 4 5 6 7 8 9 10

Michigan

Places I Visited

- [ ]
- [ ]
- [ ]
- [ ]
- [ ]
- [ ]

Date Arrived:

Time Arrived:

How long was my stay?

Where did I stay?

Who Did I stay with?

Who Did I Travel With?

How was the weather?

Best Meal

Something Funny That Happened

Something Unexpected That Happened

Highlights of my Trip

-
-
-
-
-
-

Did I Learn Anything?   Did I Make New Friends?

Why Did I Visit This State?

Notes

I Love This State (Rating 1-10)   1 2 3 4 5 6 7 8 9 10

Minnesota

Places I Visited

☐

☐

☐

☐

☐

☐

Date Arrived:

Time Arrived:

How long was my stay?

Where did I stay?

Who Did I stay with?

Who Did I Travel With?

How was the weather?

Best Meal

Something Funny That Happened

Something Unexpected That Happened

Highlights of my Trip

Did I Learn Anything? Did I Make New Friends?

Why Did I Visit This State?

Notes

I Love This State (Rating 1-10)   1 2 3 4 5 6 7 8 9 10

Mississippi

Places I Visited

- [ ]
- [ ]
- [ ]
- [ ]
- [ ]
- [ ]

Date Arrived:

Time Arrived:

How long was my stay?

Where did I stay?

Who Did I stay with?

Who Did I Travel With?

How was the weather?

Best Meal

Something Funny That Happened

Something Unexpected That Happened

_____

Highlights of my Trip

- [ ]
- [ ]
- [ ]
- [ ]
- [ ]
- [ ]

Did I Learn Anything?

_____
_____
_____

Did I Make New Friends?

_____
_____
_____

Why Did I Visit This State?

_____
_____

Notes

_____
_____

I Love This State (Rating 1-10)   1   2   3   4   5   6   7   8   9   10

Missouri

Places I Visited

- [ ]
- [ ]
- [ ]
- [ ]
- [ ]
- [ ]

Date Arrived:

Time Arrived:

How long was my stay?

Where did I stay?

Who Did I stay with?

Who Did I Travel With?

How was the weather?

Best Meal

Something Funny That Happened

Something Unexpected That Happened

Highlights of my Trip

-
-
-
-
-
-

Did I Learn Anything?   Did I Make New Friends?

Why Did I Visit This State?

Notes

I Love This State (Rating 1-10)   1 2 3 4 5 6 7 8 9 10

Montana

Places I Visited

- [ ]
- [ ]
- [ ]
- [ ]
- [ ]
- [ ]

Date Arrived:

Time Arrived:

How long was my stay?

Where did I stay?

Who Did I stay with?

Who Did I Travel With?

How was the weather?

Best Meal

Something Funny That Happened

Something Unexpected That Happened

Highlights of my Trip

-
-
-
-
-
-

Did I Learn Anything?   Did I Make New Friends?

Why Did I Visit This State?

Notes

I Love This State (Rating 1-10)   1 2 3 4 5 6 7 8 9 10

Nebraska

Places I Visited

- [ ]
- [ ]
- [ ]
- [ ]
- [ ]
- [ ]

Date Arrived:

Time Arrived:

How long was my stay?

Where did I stay?

Who Did I stay with?

Who Did I Travel With?

How was the weather?

Best Meal

Something Funny That Happened

Something Unexpected That Happened

Highlights of my Trip

- ☐
- ☐
- ☐
- ☐
- ☐
- ☐

Did I Learn Anything?	Did I Make New Friends?

Why Did I Visit This State?

Notes

I Love This State (Rating 1-10)   1 2 3 4 5 6 7 8 9 10

Nevada

Places I Visited

- [ ]
- [ ]
- [ ]
- [ ]
- [ ]
- [ ]

Date Arrived:

Time Arrived:

How long was my stay?

Where did I stay?

Who Did I stay with?

Who Did I Travel With?

How was the weather?

Best Meal

Something Funny That Happened

Something Unexpected That Happened

USA

Highlights of my Trip

- [ ]
- [ ]
- [ ]
- [ ]
- [ ]
- [ ]

Did I Learn Anything?   Did I Make New Friends?

Why Did I Visit This State?

Notes

I Love This State (Rating 1-10)   1 2 3 4 5 6 7 8 9 10

New Hampshire

Places I Visited

- [ ]
- [ ]
- [ ]
- [ ]
- [ ]
- [ ]

Date Arrived:

Time Arrived:

How long was my stay?

Where did I stay?

Who Did I stay with?

Who Did I Travel With?

How was the weather?

Best Meal

Something Funny That Happened

Something Unexpected That Happened

Highlights of my Trip

-
-
-
-
-
-

Did I Learn Anything?

Did I Make New Friends?

Why Did I Visit This State?

Notes

I Love This State (Rating 1-10)   1 2 3 4 5 6 7 8 9 10

New Jersey

Places I Visited

- [ ]
- [ ]
- [ ]
- [ ]
- [ ]
- [ ]

Date Arrived:

Time Arrived:

How long was my stay?

Where did I stay?

Who Did I stay with?

Who Did I Travel With?

How was the weather?

Best Meal

Something Funny That Happened

Something Unexpected That Happened

_____

Highlights of my Trip

☐
☐
☐
☐
☐
☐

Did I Learn Anything?   Did I Make New Friends?
_____   _____
_____   _____
_____   _____

Why Did I Visit This State?
_____
_____

Notes
_____
_____

I Love This State (Rating 1-10)   1 2 3 4 5 6 7 8 9 10

New Mexico

Places I Visited

Date Arrived:

Time Arrived:

How long was my stay?

Where did I stay?

Who Did I stay with?

Who Did I Travel With?

How was the weather?

Best Meal

Something Funny That Happened

Something Unexpected That Happened

Highlights of my Trip

Did I Learn Anything?   Did I Make New Friends?

Why Did I Visit This State?

Notes

I Love This State (Rating 1-10)   1 2 3 4 5 6 7 8 9 10

New York

Places I Visited

- [ ]
- [ ]
- [ ]
- [ ]
- [ ]
- [ ]

Date Arrived:

Time Arrived:

How long was my stay?

Where did I stay?

Who Did I stay with?

Who Did I Travel With?

How was the weather?

Best Meal

Something Funny That Happened

Something Unexpected That Happened

_____

Highlights of my Trip

☐

☐

☐

☐

☐

☐

Did I Learn Anything?   Did I Make New Friends?
_____   _____
_____   _____
_____   _____

Why Did I Visit This State?
_____
_____

Notes
_____
_____

I Love This State (Rating 1-10)   1 2 3 4 5 6 7 8 9 10

North Carolina

Places I Visited

- [ ]
- [ ]
- [ ]
- [ ]
- [ ]
- [ ]

Date Arrived:

Time Arrived:

How long was my stay?

Where did I stay?

Who Did I stay with?

Who Did I Travel With?

How was the weather?

Best Meal

Something Funny That Happened

Something Unexpected That Happened

Highlights of my Trip

- [ ]
- [ ]
- [ ]
- [ ]
- [ ]
- [ ]

Did I Learn Anything?   Did I Make New Friends?

Why Did I Visit This State?

Notes

I Love This State (Rating 1-10)   1 2 3 4 5 6 7 8 9 10

North Dakota

Places I Visited

- [ ]
- [ ]
- [ ]
- [ ]
- [ ]
- [ ]

Date Arrived:

Time Arrived:

How long was my stay?

Where did I stay?

Who Did I stay with?

Who Did I Travel With?

How was the weather?

Best Meal

Something Funny That Happened

Something Unexpected That Happened

Highlights of my Trip

-
-
-
-
-
-

Did I Learn Anything?

Did I Make New Friends?

Why Did I Visit This State?

Notes

I Love This State (Rating 1-10)   1   2   3   4   5   6   7   8   9   10

Ohio

Places I Visited

- [ ]
- [ ]
- [ ]
- [ ]
- [ ]
- [ ]

Date Arrived:

Time Arrived:

How long was my stay?

Where did I stay?

Who Did I stay with?

Who Did I Travel With?

How was the weather?

Best Meal

Something Funny That Happened

Something Unexpected That Happened

_____

Highlights of my Trip

☐

☐

☐

☐

☐

☐

Did I Learn Anything?   Did I Make New Friends?

_____   _____
_____   _____
_____   _____

Why Did I Visit This State?

_____
_____

Notes

_____
_____

I Love This State (Rating 1-10)   1 2 3 4 5 6 7 8 9 10

Oklahoma

Places I Visited

- [ ]
- [ ]
- [ ]
- [ ]
- [ ]
- [ ]

Date Arrived:

Time Arrived:

How long was my stay?

Where did I stay?

Who Did I stay with?

Who Did I Travel With?

How was the weather?

Best Meal

Something Funny That Happened

Something Unexpected That Happened

Highlights of my Trip

- [ ]
- [ ]
- [ ]
- [ ]
- [ ]
- [ ]

Did I Learn Anything?   Did I Make New Friends?

Why Did I Visit This State?

Notes

I Love This State (Rating 1-10)   1 2 3 4 5 6 7 8 9 10

Oregon

Places I Visited

Date Arrived:
Time Arrived:

How long was my stay?

Where did I stay?

Who Did I stay with?

Who Did I Travel With?

How was the weather?

Best Meal

Something Funny That Happened

Something Unexpected That Happened

Highlights of my Trip

- ☐
- ☐
- ☐
- ☐
- ☐
- ☐

Did I Learn Anything?

Did I Make New Friends?

Why Did I Visit This State?

Notes

I Love This State (Rating 1-10)   1 2 3 4 5 6 7 8 9 10

Pennsylvania

Places I Visited

- [ ]
- [ ]
- [ ]
- [ ]
- [ ]
- [ ]

Date Arrived:

Time Arrived:

How long was my stay?

Where did I stay?

Who Did I stay with?

Who Did I Travel With?

How was the weather?

Best Meal

Something Funny That Happened

Something Unexpected That Happened

Highlights of my Trip

-
-
-
-
-
-

Did I Learn Anything?   Did I Make New Friends?

Why Did I Visit This State?

Notes

I Love This State (Rating 1-10)   1 2 3 4 5 6 7 8 9 10

Rhode Island

Places I Visited

- [ ]
- [ ]
- [ ]
- [ ]
- [ ]
- [ ]

Date Arrived:

Time Arrived:

How long was my stay?

Where did I stay?

Who Did I stay with?

Who Did I Travel With?

How was the weather?

Best Meal

Something Funny That Happened

Something Unexpected That Happened

Highlights of my Trip

☐

☐

☐

☐

☐

☐

Did I Learn Anything?

Did I Make New Friends?

Why Did I Visit This State?

Notes

I Love This State (Rating 1-10) 1 2 3 4 5 6 7 8 9 10

South Carolina

Places I Visited

- [ ]
- [ ]
- [ ]
- [ ]
- [ ]
- [ ]

Date Arrived:

Time Arrived:

How long was my stay?

Where did I stay?

Who Did I stay with?

Who Did I Travel With?

How was the weather?

Best Meal

Something Funny That Happened

Something Unexpected That Happened

Highlights of my Trip

☐

☐

☐

☐

☐

☐

Did I Learn Anything?   Did I Make New Friends?

Why Did I Visit This State?

Notes

I Love This State (Rating 1-10)   1 2 3 4 5 6 7 8 9 10

South Dakota

Places I Visited

- [ ]
- [ ]
- [ ]
- [ ]
- [ ]
- [ ]

Date Arrived:

Time Arrived:

How long was my stay?

Where did I stay?

Who Did I stay with?

Who Did I Travel With?

How was the weather?

Best Meal

Something Funny That Happened

Something Unexpected That Happened

Highlights of my Trip

- ☐
- ☐
- ☐
- ☐
- ☐
- ☐

Did I Learn Anything? Did I Make New Friends?

Why Did I Visit This State?

Notes

I Love This State (Rating 1-10)   1 2 3 4 5 6 7 8 9 10

Tennessee

Places I Visited

- [ ]
- [ ]
- [ ]
- [ ]
- [ ]
- [ ]

Date Arrived:

Time Arrived:

How long was my stay?

Where did I stay?

Who Did I stay with?

Who Did I Travel With?

How was the weather?

Best Meal

Something Funny That Happened

Something Unexpected That Happened

_____

Highlights of my Trip

☐

☐

☐

☐

☐

☐

Did I Learn Anything?   Did I Make New Friends?

_____   _____
_____   _____
_____   _____

Why Did I Visit This State?

_____
_____

Notes

_____
_____

I Love This State (Rating 1-10)   1 2 3 4 5 6 7 8 9 10

Texas

Places I Visited

- [ ]
- [ ]
- [ ]
- [ ]
- [ ]
- [ ]

Date Arrived:

Time Arrived:

How long was my stay?

Where did I stay?

Who Did I stay with?

Who Did I Travel With?

How was the weather?

Best Meal

Something Funny That Happened

Something Unexpected That Happened

Highlights of my Trip

- ☐
- ☐
- ☐
- ☐
- ☐
- ☐

Did I Learn Anything?

Did I Make New Friends?

Why Did I Visit This State?

Notes

I Love This State (Rating 1-10)   1 2 3 4 5 6 7 8 9 10

Utah

Places I Visited

- [ ]
- [ ]
- [ ]
- [ ]
- [ ]
- [ ]

Date Arrived:

Time Arrived:

How long was my stay?

Where did I stay?

Who Did I stay with?

Who Did I Travel With?

How was the weather?

Best Meal

Something Funny That Happened

Something Unexpected That Happened

Highlights of my Trip

- ☐
- ☐
- ☐
- ☐
- ☐
- ☐

Did I Learn Anything?   **Did I Make New Friends?**

Why Did I Visit This State?

Notes

I Love This State (Rating 1-10)   1 2 3 4 5 6 7 8 9 10

Vermont

Places I Visited

- [ ]
- [ ]
- [ ]
- [ ]
- [ ]
- [ ]

Date Arrived:

Time Arrived:

How long was my stay?

Where did I stay?

Who Did I stay with?

Who Did I Travel With?

How was the weather?

Best Meal

Something Funny That Happened

Something Unexpected That Happened

Highlights of my Trip

-
-
-
-
-
-

Did I Learn Anything?

Did I Make New Friends?

Why Did I Visit This State?

Notes

I Love This State (Rating 1-10)   1   2   3   4   5   6   7   8   9   10

Places I Visited

Date Arrived:

Time Arrived:

How long was my stay?

Where did I stay?

Who Did I stay with?

Who Did I Travel With?

How was the weather?

Best Meal

Something Funny That Happened

Something Unexpected That Happened

Highlights of my Trip

- ☐
- ☐
- ☐
- ☐
- ☐
- ☐

Did I Learn Anything?
_____
_____
_____

Did I Make New Friends?
_____
_____
_____

Why Did I Visit This State?
_____
_____

Notes
_____
_____

I Love This State (Rating 1-10)   1 2 3 4 5 6 7 8 9 10

Washington

Places I Visited

- [ ]
- [ ]
- [ ]
- [ ]
- [ ]
- [ ]

Date Arrived:

Time Arrived:

How long was my stay?

Where did I stay?

Who Did I stay with?

Who Did I Travel With?

How was the weather?

Best Meal

Something Funny That Happened

Something Unexpected That Happened

Highlights of my Trip

- [ ]
- [ ]
- [ ]
- [ ]
- [ ]
- [ ]

Did I Learn Anything?   Did I Make New Friends?

Why Did I Visit This State?

Notes

I Love This State (Rating 1-10)   1   2   3   4   5   6   7   8   9   10

West Virginia

Places I Visited

- [ ]
- [ ]
- [ ]
- [ ]
- [ ]
- [ ]

Date Arrived:

Time Arrived:

How long was my stay?

Where did I stay?

Who Did I stay with?

Who Did I Travel With?

How was the weather?

Best Meal

Something Funny That Happened

Something Unexpected That Happened

Highlights of my Trip

- ☐
- ☐
- ☐
- ☐
- ☐
- ☐

Did I Learn Anything?   Did I Make New Friends?

Why Did I Visit This State?

Notes

I Love This State (Rating 1-10)   1 2 3 4 5 6 7 8 9 10

Wisconsin

Places I Visited

- [ ]
- [ ]
- [ ]
- [ ]
- [ ]
- [ ]

Date Arrived:
Time Arrived:

How long was my stay?

Where did I stay?

Who Did I stay with?

Who Did I Travel With?

How was the weather?

Best Meal

Something Funny That Happened

Something Unexpected That Happened

Highlights of my Trip

☐
☐
☐
☐
☐
☐

Did I Learn Anything?   Did I Make New Friends?

Why Did I Visit This State?

Notes

I Love This State (Rating 1-10)   1 2 3 4 5 6 7 8 9 10

Wyoming

Places I Visited

- [ ]
- [ ]
- [ ]
- [ ]
- [ ]
- [ ]

Date Arrived:

Time Arrived:

How long was my stay?

Where did I stay?

Who Did I stay with?

Who Did I Travel With?

How was the weather?

Best Meal

Something Funny That Happened

Something Unexpected That Happened

Highlights of my Trip

-
-
-
-
-
-

Did I Learn Anything?

Did I Make New Friends?

Why Did I Visit This State?

Notes

I Love This State (Rating 1-10)   1 2 3 4 5 6 7 8 9 10

www.ingramcontent.com/pod-product-compliance
Lightning Source LLC
Chambersburg PA
CBHW071405080526
44587CB00017B/3182